Orb Weaver wrapping grasshopper

Swallowtail Butterfly (× 2)*

*This insect has been magnified to two times its actual size. Any enlargement of the insects and spiders in this book is indicated with a *times* sign; if there is no sign, they are pictured at their actual sizes.

INSECTS AND SPIDERS

By **Lorus J.** and **Margery Milne**

Illustrated by **Claire Phipps**

Doubleday

PUBLISHED BY DOUBLEDAY
a division of
Bantam Doubleday Dell Publishing Group, Inc.
666 Fifth Avenue, New York, New York 10103

DOUBLEDAY
and the portrayal of an anchor with a dolphin
are trademarks of Doubleday,
a division of Bantam Doubleday Dell
Publishing Group, Inc.

Library of Congress Cataloging-in-Publication Data
Milne, Lorus Johnson, 1912–
    Insects and spiders / by Lorus J. and Margery
Milne; illustrated by Claire Phipps.—1st ed.
        p.   cm.
    Summary: An introduction to the physical
characteristics, habits, and natural environment of
different types of insects and spiders.
    1. Insects—Juvenile literature. 2. Spiders—
Juvenile literature. [1. Insects. 2. Spiders.] I.
Milne, Margery Joan Greene, 1914–. II. Phipps,
Claire, ill. III. Title.
QL467.2.M55 1991
595.7—dc20   89-29385   CIP   AC

ISBN 0-385-26396-1

Bees

Scorpion

Velvet Mite (× 1(

Tarantula

Mite (× 10)

"Ours" Is an Insect World

This world we claim as ours is really a world of insects. They have dominated it for millions of years. Insects have been on Earth 350 million years. We can trace our human ancestors only 3.5 million years into the past. Insects, with spiders close behind, were the earliest known land animals and the first flying animals.

Insects are found everywhere in the world: tundra, water, soil, plants, even inside the bodies of other animals. More than a million different kinds have been given names, which is more than all other animals combined. Those who observe these creatures find them as beautiful and fascinating as flowers or birds.

All over the globe the six-legged creatures help flowering plants to set seeds and produce fruits. A whole array of animals, from fish to mammals, rely on insects as food. Without them our world would be very different.

Spiders are often mistaken for insects. They and their close kin—the mites, ticks, and scorpions—belong to a different class of animals called arachnids. Spiders are found anywhere on land, even remote islands at sea and at 22,000 feet above sea level. There are about 30,000 different kinds. They include skilled weavers with silk sometimes stronger than steel. Spiders prey on insect pests and are used in medical research.

What Makes an Insect an Insect and a Spider a Spider?

An insect is an invertebrate animal. This means it does not have a backbone. The body of an adult insect is divided into three parts: the head, the thorax, and the abdomen. The head bears the antennae. It also has the mouth parts. Different insects have different kinds of mouth parts. Beetles have jaws. Mosquitoes have piercing, sucking mouth parts with daggerlike structures. Bees and wasps have biting and lapping mouth parts. Butterflies and moths have coiled, tonguelike structures for sipping. Each insect has mouth parts that suit its needs.

There are two kinds of eyes on insects' heads: simple and compound. The simple eyes are sensitive to light. The compound eyes can see detail because they have many lenses.

All insects have six legs. Many have one or more pairs of wings. In beetles and grasshoppers, the forewings are like armor. The hind wings are folded, fanlike, under them. Some primitive insects, like lice and fleas, have no wings at all.

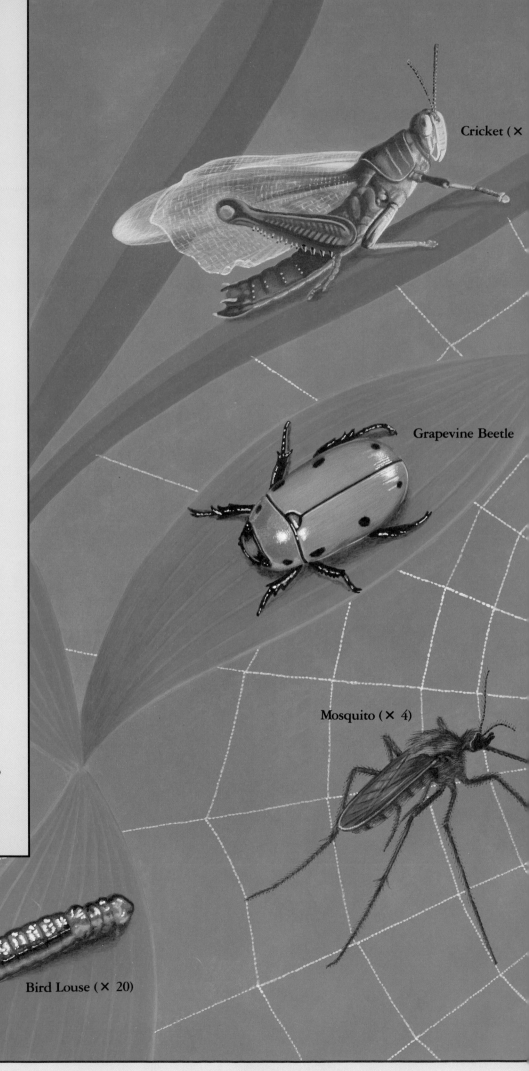

Cricket (×

Grapevine Beetle

Mosquito (× 4)

Bird Louse (× 20)

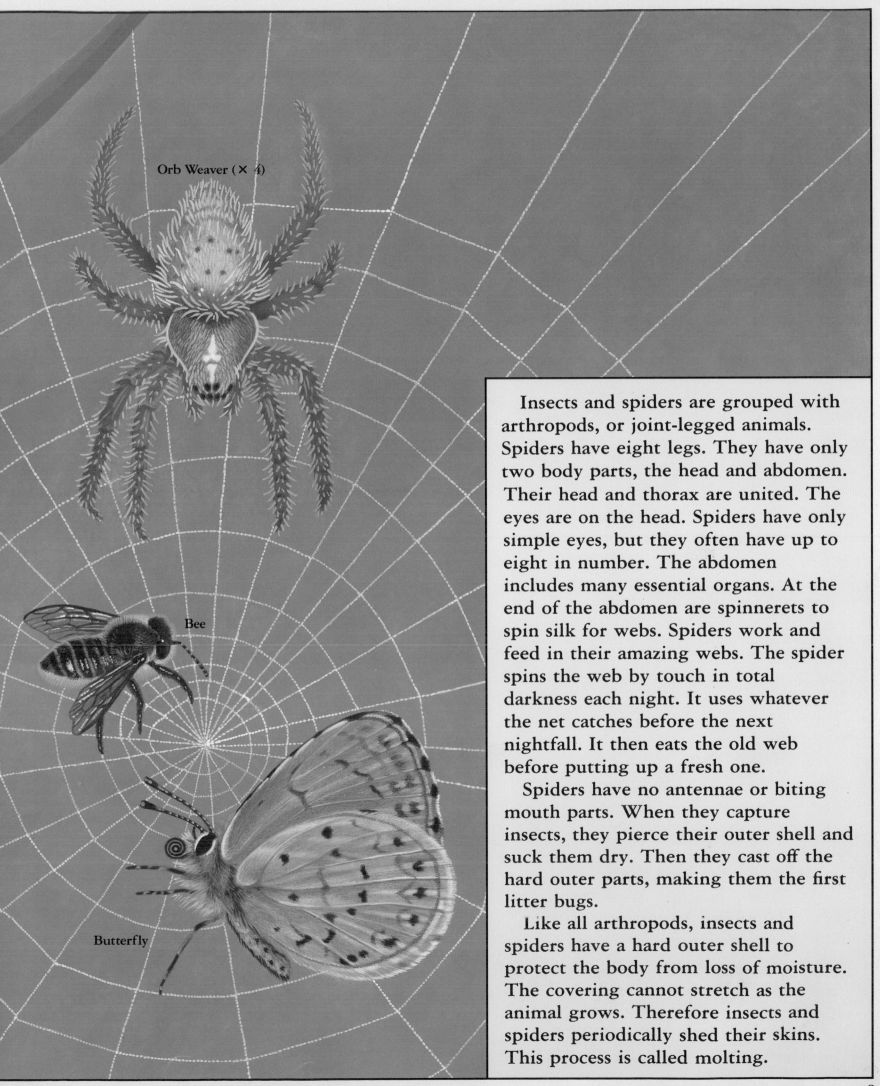

Orb Weaver (✕ 4)

Bee

Butterfly

Insects and spiders are grouped with arthropods, or joint-legged animals. Spiders have eight legs. They have only two body parts, the head and abdomen. Their head and thorax are united. The eyes are on the head. Spiders have only simple eyes, but they often have up to eight in number. The abdomen includes many essential organs. At the end of the abdomen are spinnerets to spin silk for webs. Spiders work and feed in their amazing webs. The spider spins the web by touch in total darkness each night. It uses whatever the net catches before the next nightfall. It then eats the old web before putting up a fresh one.

Spiders have no antennae or biting mouth parts. When they capture insects, they pierce their outer shell and suck them dry. Then they cast off the hard outer parts, making them the first litter bugs.

Like all arthropods, insects and spiders have a hard outer shell to protect the body from loss of moisture. The covering cannot stretch as the animal grows. Therefore insects and spiders periodically shed their skins. This process is called molting.

Life cycle of Monarch Butterfly

Female laying eggs (× 2)

Pupa

Egg (× 20)

Newly hatched caterpillar (× 20)

Caterpillar beginning metamorphosis (× 2)

Chrysalis

Pupa transforming into chrysalis

Butterfly emerging from chrysalis

Life Cycles of Insects and Spiders

The young of some insects, such as silverfish and springtails, look very much like the adults. However, most young insects do not resemble the adults at all.

Creeping caterpillars become beautiful butterflies. Soft white grubs change into beetles clad in armor. Underwater creatures like dragonfly nymphs shed their skins and suddenly are airborne dragonflies.

The life story of an individual insect is called its life cycle or metamorphosis. Most insects do not become larger as they grow. Instead, they pass through various creeping stages. Insects that go through four stages, including a pupal stage, are said to undergo complete metamorphosis. The butterfly undergoes complete metamorphosis. It lays eggs which hatch into creeping forms with chewing mouth parts. These are caterpillars or larvae. In this stage the insect feeds and grows. When the active caterpillar is fully grown, it sheds its skin and transforms into an inactive pupa. This is called a chrysalis in the case of a butterfly. During this resting stage the pupa transforms into an adult. When the chrysalis is mature, you can see the wings and legs of the future butterfly through its transparent skin. The chrysalis then splits open and the butterfly crawls out. At first its wings are shriveled. Then they rapidly expand and harden. The adult winged butterfly is then ready for flight. The mouth parts are no longer suited for chewing leaves but for sipping nectar from flowers. This life cycle is typical of moths, bees, wasps, ants, beetles, and flies. In beetles the larva stage is often called a grub.

Some insects have only three stages in their life cycle: egg, larva, and adult. This is an incomplete metamorphosis. They have no pupal, or resting stage. Instead of being called a caterpillar, the larva is called a nymph. This life cycle is typical of dragonflies, true bugs, mayflies, grasshoppers, and cicadas. In grasshoppers the young, or nymphs, resemble the adults but have no wings. In other insects, like dragonflies and cicadas, the young do not resemble the adults at all. Young dragonflies are wingless, crawling creatures called naiads that live in ponds and streams. When naiads are fully developed, they crawl up above the surface of the water. They then attach themselves to plants, and unfold their wings to become winged adults.

A mayfly naiad eats a lifetime supply of food. It lives underwater, scraping food from the surface of rocks. When it has digested all the food, the insect rises to the surface of the water and bursts into the air. At exactly that moment the wings suddenly expand and the mayfly flits to the nearest cattail or overhanging tree. There it waits for further changes that will make it an adult. It will never eat again but will join an aerial ballet in search

Dragonfly

Mayfly naiad (× 2)

Mosquito larva

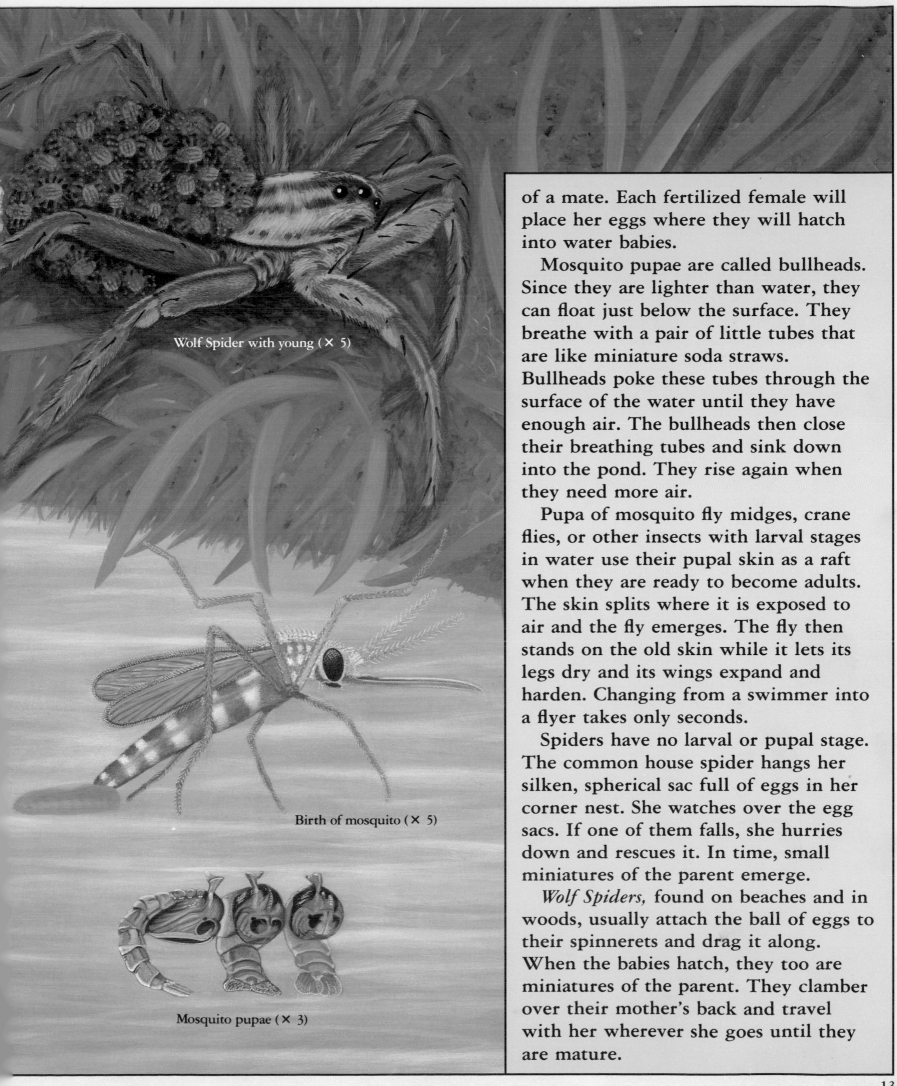

Wolf Spider with young (× 5)

Birth of mosquito (× 5)

Mosquito pupae (× 3)

of a mate. Each fertilized female will place her eggs where they will hatch into water babies.

Mosquito pupae are called bullheads. Since they are lighter than water, they can float just below the surface. They breathe with a pair of little tubes that are like miniature soda straws. Bullheads poke these tubes through the surface of the water until they have enough air. The bullheads then close their breathing tubes and sink down into the pond. They rise again when they need more air.

Pupa of mosquito fly midges, crane flies, or other insects with larval stages in water use their pupal skin as a raft when they are ready to become adults. The skin splits where it is exposed to air and the fly emerges. The fly then stands on the old skin while it lets its legs dry and its wings expand and harden. Changing from a swimmer into a flyer takes only seconds.

Spiders have no larval or pupal stage. The common house spider hangs her silken, spherical sac full of eggs in her corner nest. She watches over the egg sacs. If one of them falls, she hurries down and rescues it. In time, small miniatures of the parent emerge.

Wolf Spiders, found on beaches and in woods, usually attach the ball of eggs to their spinnerets and drag it along. When the babies hatch, they too are miniatures of the parent. They clamber over their mother's back and travel with her wherever she goes until they are mature.

Successful Beetles

W herever an insect of any kind can live, several kinds of beetles are usually at home. They outnumber all other kinds of insects.

The secret of their success is that beetles are nearly indestructible. Their heads and bodies are protected by armorlike plates. The first pair of wings also acts as armor. In the air, beetles are slow, but on land they travel easily. If a flying beetle crashes into an obstacle, it simply folds its wings and continues along the ground on its sturdy legs. If the obstacle on the ground is the bark of a tree or a branch with edible leaves, the beetle may use its strong jaws to cut a passageway or to free fragments of foliage to eat.

The most active beetles are often the most brilliantly colored. Shiny green *Tiger Beetles* skitter like jewels along woodland paths. Bronze ones frequent open grasslands and beaches, where they pursue other small insects.

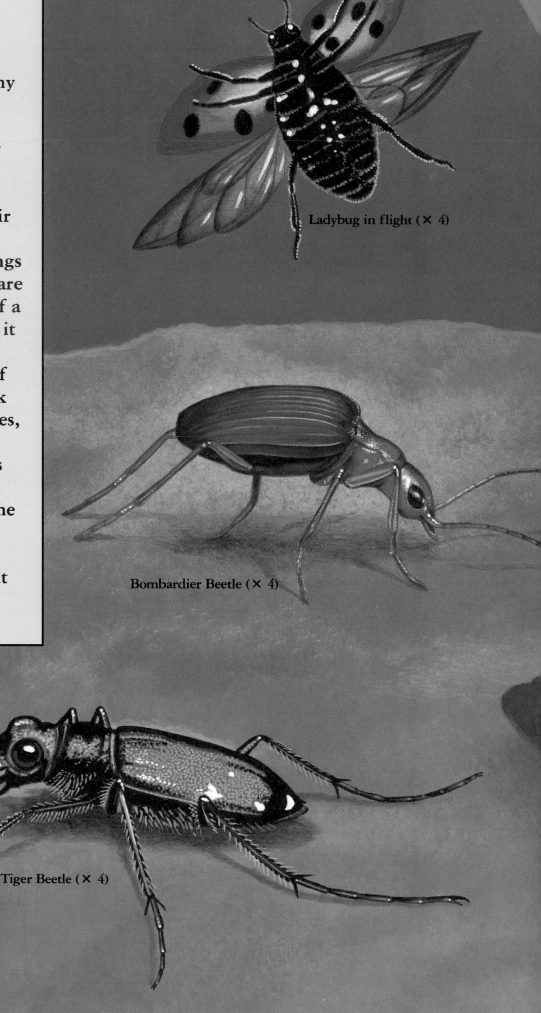

Ladybug in flight (✕ 4)

Bombardier Beetle (✕ 4)

Tiger Beetle (✕ 4)

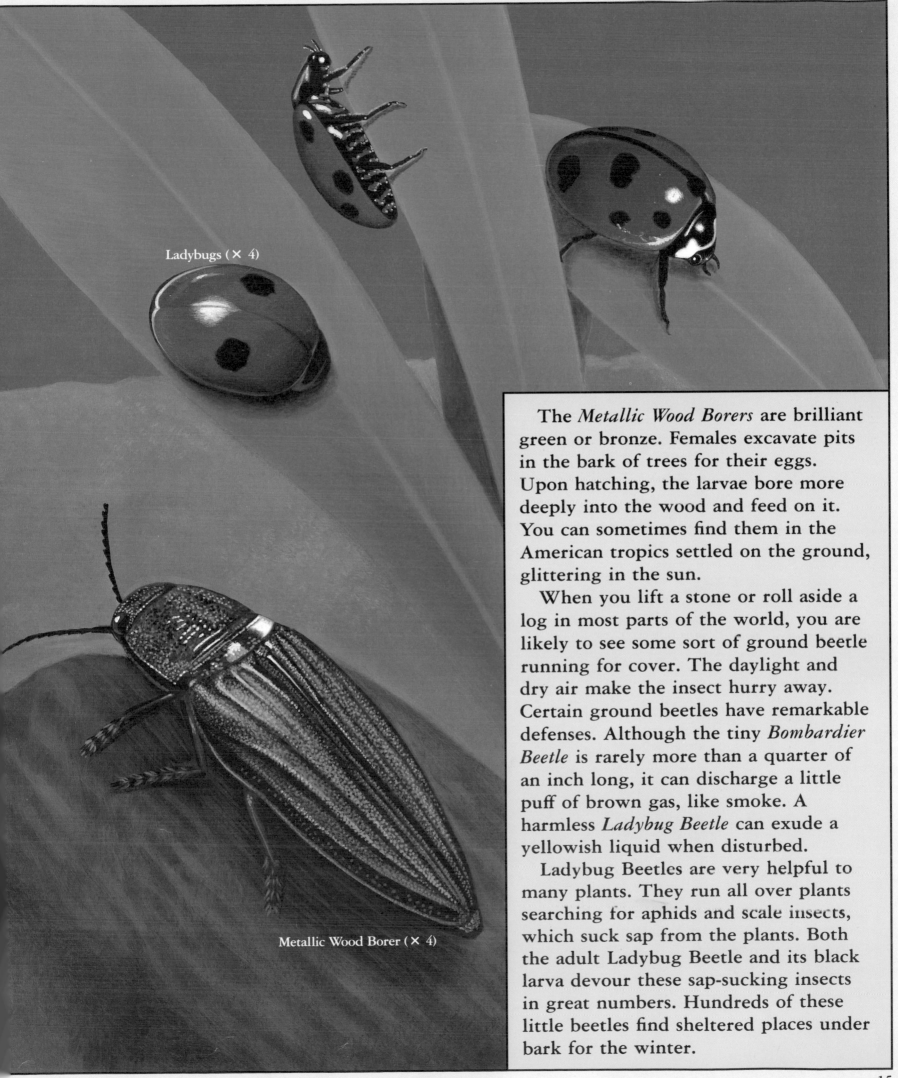

Ladybugs (× 4)

Metallic Wood Borer (× 4)

The *Metallic Wood Borers* are brilliant green or bronze. Females excavate pits in the bark of trees for their eggs. Upon hatching, the larvae bore more deeply into the wood and feed on it. You can sometimes find them in the American tropics settled on the ground, glittering in the sun.

When you lift a stone or roll aside a log in most parts of the world, you are likely to see some sort of ground beetle running for cover. The daylight and dry air make the insect hurry away. Certain ground beetles have remarkable defenses. Although the tiny *Bombardier Beetle* is rarely more than a quarter of an inch long, it can discharge a little puff of brown gas, like smoke. A harmless *Ladybug Beetle* can exude a yellowish liquid when disturbed.

Ladybug Beetles are very helpful to many plants. They run all over plants searching for aphids and scale insects, which suck sap from the plants. Both the adult Ladybug Beetle and its black larva devour these sap-sucking insects in great numbers. Hundreds of these little beetles find sheltered places under bark for the winter.

Fireflies, or *Lightning Bugs,* are beetles with the amazing ability to produce light without heat. They use their brightly lit organs to wink coded messages in the dark to find mates. The male Firefly flies back and forth above a meadow, using his large compound eyes to scan the surrounding scene. He flashes a message to advertise for a mate. When she sees it, a female of the same kind responds with her light. The male then comes in for a landing on the leaf where she rests.

Click Beetles, also called *Fire Beetles,* have brightly lit spots. They get their name because they make a clicking sound when they flip into the air after being turned over on their backs. They live in tropical Central and South America or some Southern states, including Florida and Texas. A Fire Beetle uses its lighting system to attract a mate, but it cannot wink the lighted spots on and off in a code the way a Firefly does.

Forests and fields with woody shrubs are homes for Click Beetles, Metallic Wood Borers, and the beetles with extremely long antennae known as *Longicorns.* The antennae of one type of

Pyralis Firefly (× 2)

Black Pine Sawyer

Fire Beetle (× 2)

16

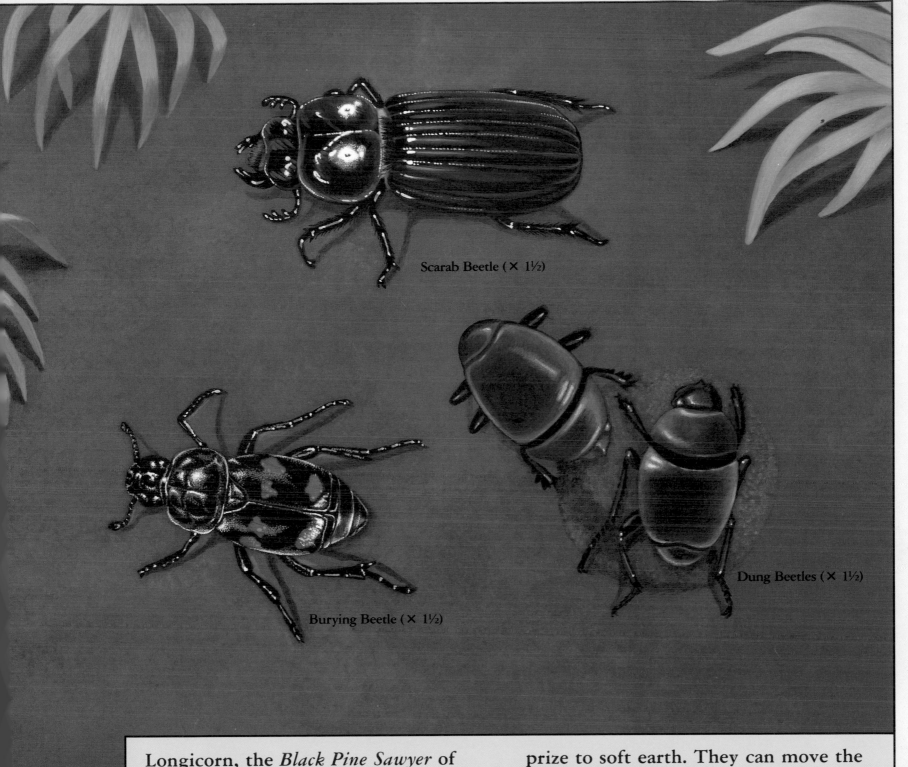

Scarab Beetle (× 1½)

Burying Beetle (× 1½)

Dung Beetles (× 1½)

Longicorn, the *Black Pine Sawyer* of Eastern North America, are two inches long on a male whose main body is only one inch long. No one knows why.

Scarab Beetles have clublike antennae. They include the *Dung Beetles,* which scavenge and rear their grublike larvae in animal waste. These beetles recycle waste and make it useful as fertilizer for plants.

Burying Beetles live together like families. Adults crawl under a dead mouse, sparrow, or snake. They then lift it a part at a time and transport the prize to soft earth. They can move the body up to fifteen feet away. The beetles then push out the earth underneath the animal, burying the body in the ground. The animal will provide food for the adult beetles and their young. Young and adults communicate with scratchy sounds. Both parents stay with their larvae until the larvae are ready to become pupae. The males of other cold-blooded animals rarely help rear their young.

Beetles will be our companions on Earth as long as humankind exists.

Beaked Bugs

Beaked-bearers are insects with sharp, beaklike mouth parts that must suck juices from plants and animals for food. They inhabit every continent except Australia. Some, such as *Spittlebugs,* or *Froghoppers,* live in fields or woodlands standing on weeds or grass or pine branches. They drink a plant's juice while blowing bubbles to create froth. The bubbles look like beaten egg whites and are the Froghoppers' homes.

The Froghopper must constantly make more bubbles to replenish the froth, for its body cannot stand dry air. If the froth is pushed away, the insect briefly crouches in a froglike manner. It then frees its beak from the plant and quickly jumps on its large hind legs into a new site, where it creates a new frothy shelter.

Leafhoppers and *Treehoppers* leap like Froghoppers when threatened and suck the juices of plants, but they do not produce froth. The scarlet and green Leafhoppers of Northeastern North America are beautifully colored.

Scale Insects hide from hungry birds. Soon after each young Scale Insect leaves its mother, it finds a place of its

Leafhopper (× 2)

Froghopper (× 2)

Giant Water Bug (× 2)

Treehopper (× 2)

Cottony Cushion Scale (× 2)

Backswimmer (× 2)

own on a plant stem where it sips the plant juice. It then covers itself completely with a spittle excretion. The *Cottony Cushion Scale* looks like a mass of cottony wax.

The largest of the beak-bearers are the *Giant Water Bugs.* Some of them are four and a half inches long. These Giant Water Bugs live in shallow fresh water. They creep or swim slowly among submerged vegetation and ambush fish, tadpoles, or other insects. Most of these bugs are tropical, but several North American species live as far north as Canada. They used to be known as "electric-light bugs" because so many were attracted to streetlights. Now these bugs are in danger. The shallow waters from which they came have been filled in, destroying their habitats.

The *Backswimmer* spends almost its entire life upside down suspended in water. The Backswimmer can raise or lower itself in the water. It keeps its two longest legs (the middle pair) extended like sculling oars. It turns and rows about, looking for insects that have fallen into the pond. The Backswimmer pokes its beak into its prey and drinks the prey's juices. It can use its beak to stab enemies and is called the *Water Wasp* in Europe.

Parasites and Primitives

Among creatures great and small it is often the most inconspicuous ones that have had the greatest impact on civilization. Many of the insects that have plagued humans for centuries are indeed very small.

Lice, fleas, mosquitoes, and other insects that feed on blood are all sensitive to body temperature. They choose warm-blooded animals as hosts to feed on.

In some primitive societies, medicine men check for lice on people who seem sick. As long as they can find lice on the sick person's head, medicine men know a patient has a normal body temperature and may soon recover. A fever makes parasites such as the louse uncomfortable and they move to a new victim.

Dogs become hosts to the *Dog Flea,* and cats to the *Cat Flea.* Cat Fleas will live on dogs only if the desired host, the cat, is not around.

Several different parasites once afflicted only wild animals but now plague humans. The *Human Flea* is one of these. The Human Flea, of which there are six thousand kinds on Earth, grows no more than a quarter inch in length. It has the unusual ability to leap a foot or more into the air, from one host to another. The Human Flea became a performer in a "flea circus," dancing under a tiny paper cone pulling a minute cart when harnessed with a very fine wire.

Human Flea (× 20)

Cat Flea (× 20)

Hog Louse (× 20)

Earwig (× 1½)

Silverfish (× 2)

Thrip (× 20)

A louse is faithful to the host on which it feeds, from the louse's immaturity to adulthood. *Hog Lice* and *Human Lice* feed repeatedly, making a fresh puncture each time. *Chewing Lice* infest chickens and are much larger. *Wingless Book Lice* infest many houses, where they feed on the glue of book bindings.

Earwigs grow big enough to be seen easily. The *Common Earwig* has successfully invaded North America and spread to New England. The tip of its abdomen, like that of any earwig, bears a pair of pincers which are used to fight. The *Seaside Earwig* will grasp a beach flea and twist its flexible body to bring the victim near its mouth to be eaten.

The *Silverfish* is about the most primitive pest in a household. It is a half inch long and can be found worldwide. It takes about two years to grow from a nymph to an adult.

Among the world's most bizarre small insects are the *Thrips,* or *Snow Fleas.* These tiny insects creep into flowers and curl their bodies over their backs as they crawl on very short legs. They are the size of a small particle of "dirt." In winter they gather in groups, appearing as dark, blue motes forming dark patches on the snow. These Snow Fleas ride the surface film on maple sap that has collected in buckets. The *Seashore Springtail* is inconspicuous most of the year. In warm weather, though, huge clusters of these creatures are often found all along the North American coast, nestled in scattered air pockets among beach litter when the tide is especially h

Look-Alikes

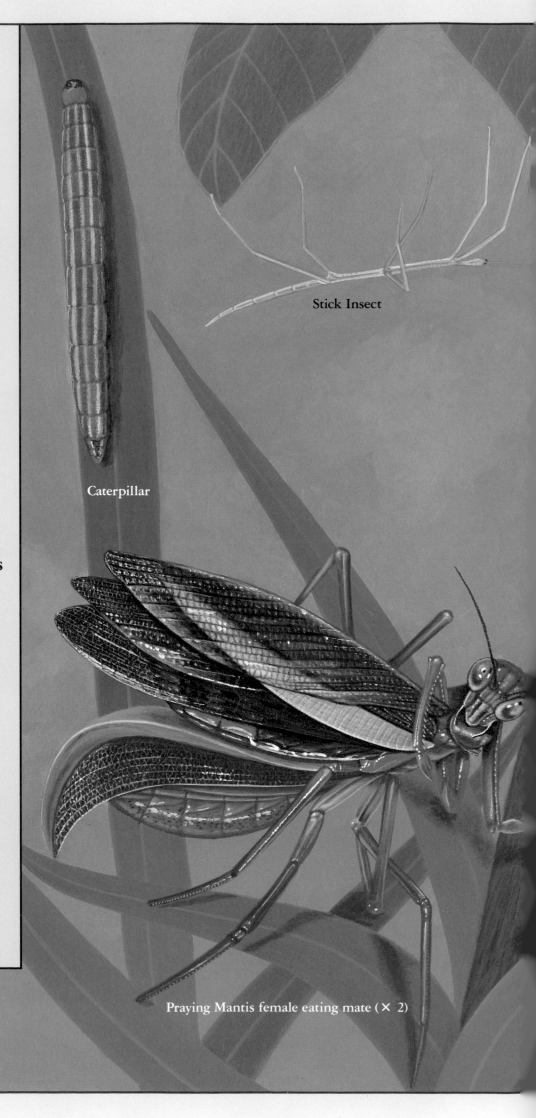

Some creatures are strong, well armed, and able to resist attack. Others must find other ways to protect themselves. Nature is full of copy cats. Many fool predators by looking like other creatures. Some masquerade as an inedible part of the background, such as caterpillars that resemble twigs. As long as they remain still, they are not discovered. But once they move, they can be discovered by a bird or another insect.

A *Mantis* can look like leaves or stems. It will stand for hours, with its wings folded over its back and its grasping appendages held beneath its head. This motionless pose has inspired people to call it the *"Praying" Mantis.*

Strange tropical Mantises often look like dead, drying leaves as long as they stand still. A Mantis can stay motionless for an extraordinarily long time. It can wait for weeks if necessary between one meal and the next. While still, it keeps an eye out for a meal. The Mantis turns slowly to face any potential victim. In fact, it is the only insect that can turn its head enough to look over its own shoulder. The Mantis may take a slow step or two, but it moves no faster than a leaf might blow. A male Mantis must approach a potential mate slowly and cautiously. Otherwise she will eat him.

Tropical Stick Insects look like sticks or twigs. They flutter if shaken from a tree, but when they land on another tree they become still again. A few of

Caterpillar

Stick Insect

Praying Mantis female eating mate (× 2)

Leaf Insect

Treehoppers

Glass-Wing Butterfly

these insects in the rain forests of South America and Africa can be up to thirteen inches long.

The bright green *Leaf Insects* of Southern and Southeastern Asia are related to Stick Insects. Leaf Insects visit the cacao trees disguised as leaves. Each has an amazingly broad, green abdomen and leaflike expansions of its legs. Leaf Insects sometimes don't recognize another of their own kind. They have been known to take a bite of each other while standing motionless side by side.

Treehoppers often have a hornlike projection above their bodies. This makes them look like thorns as they cling to a branch and sip sap from it.

Some insects are almost transparent and seem invisible. This is another effective camouflage. *Glass-Wing Butterflies* of the American tropics can scarcely be seen in flight because their surroundings show right through their wings. If they settle on a flower, one can see the flower through the wings. Even when they hold their wings together over their back, they are almost invisible.

Insects that are bad-tasting, smelly, or poisonous, or that sting or bite, do not need camouflage. Mammals and insect-eating birds learn quickly to avoid these insects. Certain nonpoisonous insects protect themselves by looking like other insects that are poisonous. The bitter-tasting *Monarch Butterfly* has a smaller look-alike called the *Viceroy Butterfly.* The American Bluejay won't eat Monarchs or Viceroys.

Love Songs and Other Sounds

Insects' sounds filled the earth long before frogs croaked or birds sang. Most of these sounds are made by a male inviting a female of the same kind to come close. The first of these insects may have been the grasshoppers, crickets, and katydids. The cicadas were not far behind, and soon they became the noisiest of all.

In the rain forests of Malaya and Borneo, you can hear the cicada's sound at the break of day and at day's end. In Australia the primitive *Alpine Cicada* hides beneath bark all day and comes out only at night. Most of the world's 1,500 kinds of cicada are large, heavy-bodied insects. The *Periodical Cicada,* or the *Seventeen-Year Locust,* spends seventeen years underground. The burrowing immature nymphs feed on sap in tree roots for all these years before they emerge from the soil. They emerge before sunrise and begin their shrill calling.

Green Valley Grasshopper (× 2)

Katydid (× 2)

Grasshopper (× 2)

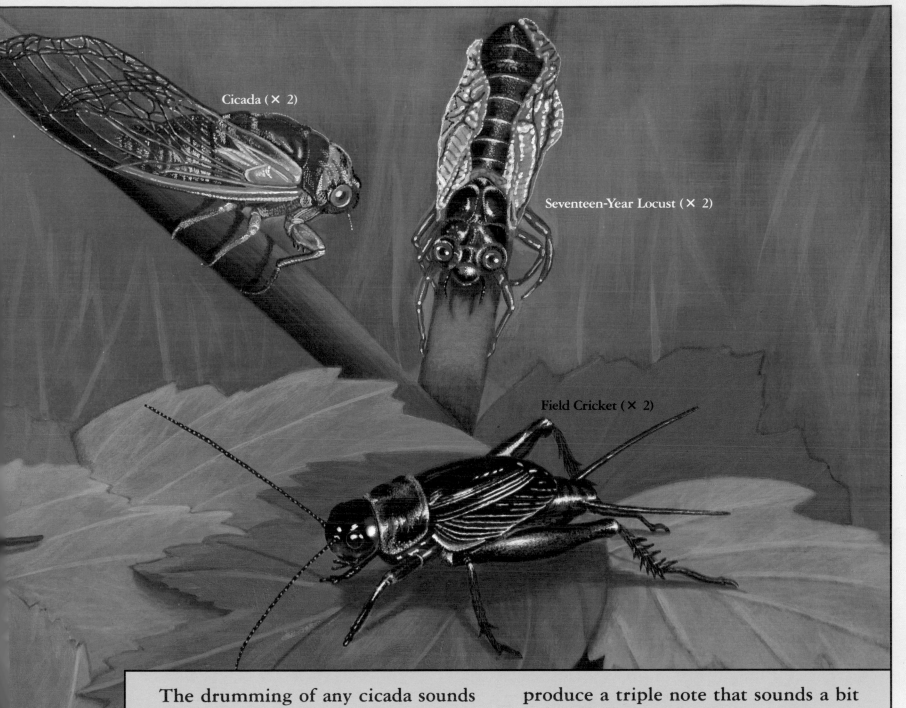

Cicada (× 2)

Seventeen-Year Locust (× 2)

Field Cricket (× 2)

The drumming of any cicada sounds different from the rasping and trilling calls of leaping crickets, katydids, and grasshoppers. Each cricket, katydid, or other long-horn grasshopper has a filelike row of teeth on the under surface of the upper wing. This row of teeth rests against a hard, crosswise ridge on the upper surface of the lower wing. The insect shrugs its shoulders at high speed to produce a note. The mate hears the sound with a small earlike organ at the surface of the front leg, just beyond the knee joint.

The male *Common Black Field Cricket* enthusiastically attracts his mate. He has 142 teeth on his file. He uses it to produce a triple note that sounds a bit like "Please come here!" at a pitch close to the top of the piano scale. When a female does appear, the male dances around her and smells her perfume. He then changes his call to the same frequency as though repeating, "Lovely, lovely, lovely." To make his summoning call, he strikes only about 62 teeth on his file. His single courtship message uses about 92 teeth in one continuous chirp.

The crickets, grasshoppers, and katydids offer their music as the summer season's last symphony orchestra. Their songs ring through the air of autumn.

Fantastic Butterflies

No cabbage patch in America is too small to attract a *Cabbage Butterfly.* It was introduced from Europe to Quebec in 1860 and has spread from coast to coast. In any garden between spring and fall, a white male with dark spots on his forewings rises and falls among the tall plants, stopping for an occasional sip of nectar. When his antennae pick up the scent of a female, he quickly flies an inch away from her. He then turns his antennae toward her. She opens her wings and closes them again above her back, helping to waft her perfume toward him.

In North America the widespread *Tiger Swallowtail* has two types of females, the light yellow phase and the dark phase, in the Southeast, but only one, the light yellow, elsewhere. The paler Tiger females resemble the males but they are scarce in the South. Males have been observed to pursue only females like themselves. But birds prey on the lighter phase butterflies, as the darker phase resembles the untasty *Pipevine Swallowtail.*

The American tropics have whole families of butterflies that predators cannot eat. With their long, slender bodies and extended, rounded wings, these butterflies can be seen quivering through rain forest clearings. One familiar species is the *Zebra Butterfly* of southernmost Florida and the West Indies. As night falls, dozens snuggle

Tiger Swallowtail Butterfly

Cabbage Butterfly

Zebra Butterfly

Morpho Butterfly

Monarch caterpillar

Monarch Butterfly

together through the fading light on a favorite branch until sunrise. Probably the combined odor of the group repels predators.

High in the rain forests are butterflies that actually reflect sunlight like mirrors, making them appear shiny blue. The scales on the wings break up the color, giving the effect of a prism. The great *Morpho Butterflies* display for mates in this way by coasting through the vegetation and sometimes flapping.

The amazing wings of these flashing Morphos were once used in jewelry. Brazil now has a law forbidding the capture of butterflies for this purpose. Some Morpho wings still appear in jewelry, but they come from insects raised in captivity.

The most outstanding traveler in North America is the sturdy *Monarch Butterfly.* Each autumn vast numbers wing southward from southern Canada and the northern United States all the way to Florida, the Gulf states, California, and Mexico. They travel in huge hordes of thousands and rest in evergreen trees. Each day they venture out for dew and nectar.

Most of the Monarchs are heading toward the Mexican mountaintops. However, the far western Monarchs may settle for the cold months at Pacific Grove in California.

From all these wintering sites, the females head north again, arriving in spring wherever they can find young milkweed plants. There the eggs are laid where the caterpillars have their favorite food plant.

Marvelous Moths

Most moths are night fliers with colors not as bright as those in butterflies. Yet some day-flying moths have bright colors. Their antennae are often feathery, unlike the knobbed ones of butterflies.

You may have been lucky enough to see the magnificent *Luna Moth.* These are common to many suburban communities. In these same places a dozen other *Giant Silkworm Moths* of different kinds may appear during a typical summer. They fly high into the treetops soon after emerging from their cocoons. Most of them come out of tough, egg-shaped cocoons lying on the ground below maple and sycamore and basswood trees. As caterpillars grow, they emerge as brownish yellow *Polyphemus Moths* and climb high above

Polyphemus Moth caterpillar

Polyphemus Moth

Cocoon

Cecropia Moth caterpillar

Luna Moth

Silkworm cocoon

Atlas Moth

the earth in preparation for their first flight.

Caterpillars of the *Cecropia Moth* emerge from eggs left by the mother on ash, elm, and willow trees. When fully grown, the caterpillar descends from its tree to spin its cocoon. Its cocoon encloses a strong branch to support it all winter, while the pupa inside turns into a moth.

The Giant Silkworm Moths come from the biggest cocoons with the most silk. The adults include the most spectacular night fliers all over the world. The *Atlas Moth* of Asia, with a wingspan as great as ten inches, may have a larger wing area than any other insect.

A surprising array of Giant Silkworm Moths wear impressive giant eyespots on their wings. These can frighten away a bird, lizard, or monkey. Even the little *Io Moth* of North America, with only a three-inch wingspan, can scare predators with its eyespots. Its

caterpillar has an even stronger defense
—branching, poisonous spines like
miniature Christmas trees cover it.

Underwing Moths have no such
defense mechanisms and must be more
alert. They belong to mothdom's
largest family. Their fine hearing
organs on each side of the body alert
the moths to the approach of an echo-
ranging bat. When a bat nears, down
plunges the moth to hide silently.

Tiger Moths are day-flying moths. The
best known of these is the snow-white
Woolly Bear Moth, the adult form of the
Woolly Bear Caterpillar. According to
folklore, this insect forecasts the
severity of the winter, depending on
the number of segments concealed by
bristly, black hairs: the more black
hairs, the more severe the weather. No
one, though, has any scientific evidence
for this. "Hurrying along like a
caterpillar in the fall" is a New

Io Moth caterpillar

Io Moth

Cutworm

Sweetheart Underwing Moth

White-lined Sphinx Moth

Woolly Bear caterpillar

Woolly Bear Moth

Cocoon

England saying. Many a Woolly Bear is still hungry when spring weather wakes it from hibernation. Its outer covering is fresh and clean, even though it was slept in during the winter. The larva feeds on roadside weeds. When ready the larva spins a cocoon, stiffening it with bristles from its outer coat and starting a pupa.

Some of the *Hawk Moths* are active during the day, visiting flowers. They flit on strong, pointed wings and hover like a hummingbird while they sip nectar.

Because moths eat leaves, they can endanger the survival of plants. However, by eating away at higher foliage, they help plants closer to the ground by allowing more sunlight to warm the soil and reach the lower plants.

Giant Western Crane Fly

Crane Fly

Net-winged Midge (× 2)

Common Water Strider

Waterways

You have probably seen insects walk on water and wondered why they didn't sink. Many insects that walk on water use well-waxed, hair-booted feet that the water cannot wet. The best known of them are the *Water Striders.* Water Striders have four long legs stretching out to the sides and a shorter pair under the head. Each foot presses the water surface and makes a dimple there, but fine waxy bristles do not let the foot fall through the surface film. The Strider stands chiefly on its hind and foremost legs. It uses its middle pair of legs as oars.

On quiet days Striders may go far from shore. But if a breeze springs up, they hurry back to the calmer waters near the bank. Rain and winter drive the Striders from the water to land but all active stages of the Water Strider's life are spent on the water.

Other insects that spend their days with outstretched feet may rest safely on the water film. Small gnats and midges flit from place to place on the pond. Even large *Crane Flies* settle with surprising grace upon the water's skin. If one is hurt while resting on the water surface, Water Striders gather around it and eat what is left.

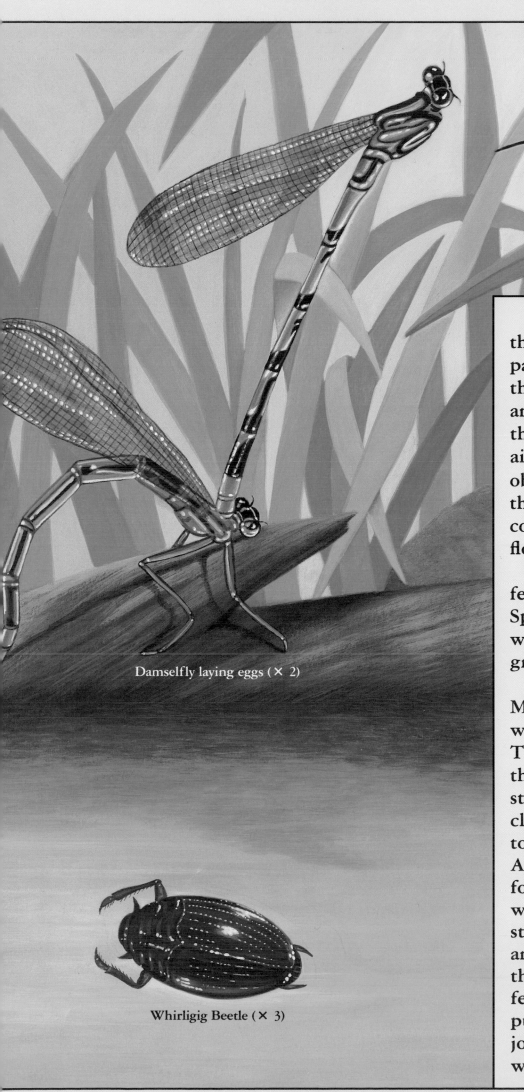

Fungus Gnat (× 3)

Damselfly laying eggs (× 2)

Whirligig Beetle (× 3)

Whirligig Beetles can propel themselves at a fast pace. Their short, paddlelike feet dip into the water but their bodies stay dry. The eyes and antennae of a Whirligig stay exactly at the waterline, so the insect can see in air and water. It looks for ripples from objects ahead or to the sides. This way the Whirligig can zig and zag without colliding with other Whirligigs or floating obstacles.

Sometimes Whirligigs disturb feeding *Blue-Gray Springtails.* These Springtails creep or bounce over the water surface. They feed on pollen grains blown onto the water.

Some insects lay their eggs in water. Male and female *Damselflies* wrap their wings around themselves like a cloak. This provides a bubble of air. They then crawl down into the water to a stone or stem. The male uses a pair of claspers at the end of his long abdomen to hold his mate by her slender neck. After the eggs are fertilized and ready for laying, the pair return to the water's edge. The female backs down a stem into the water. The male holds on and remains above the surface. When the eggs have been deposited, the female starts upward while the male pulls. He flutters his wings until their joint efforts bring the female out of the water. She dries off and they fly away.

Two-Winged Aviators

Flies have become firmly established on this planet. There are more than 86,000 species known worldwide and about 16,300 in North America. Most flies depend on liquid food. Their mouth parts are varied and versatile for sucking food. Flies all have one pair of wings. Some can beat their wings 2,000 times a second or more. Flies' larvae are called maggots.

Bee Flies often stand still on a daisy, with their wings outstretched, as they sip nectar. Their great curved, compound eyes with a thousand facets in different directions help warn the fly of predators. The Bee Fly combines vision with scent to recognize a real bee or wasp that comes to the same flower. It then follows the other insect to its nest to lay an egg where there will be a ready food supply.

Bigger eyes and better vision allow a *Robber Fly* to attack other insects. It forces the beaklike extension of its head into the body of the victim. It even attacks people, but if you stay still you should be able to avoid attack.

Female *Mosquitoes* and *Blackflies* also like people. The female needs the chemical elements from blood to produce a large number of eggs.

Midge larvae tell us that streams and lakes are polluted. They are known as "bloodworms" because of their bright

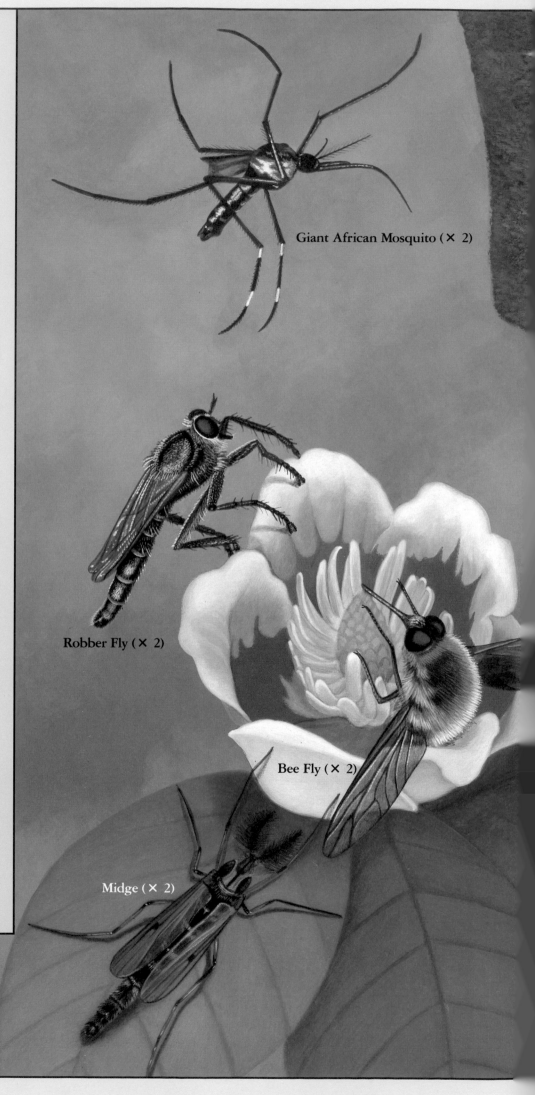

Giant African Mosquito (× 2)

Robber Fly (× 2)

Bee Fly (× 2)

Midge (× 2)

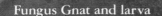

Hover Fly (× 2)

Rosy Red Aphid (× 2)

California Seaweed Fly (× 4)

red color that is easy to see. They scavenge in the bottom muck, where decayed bacteria have used up all the dissolved oxygen, a condition that is a sure sign of pollution. They grow up into harmless midges that we see dancing in the air above bushes and trees.

Rotting vegetable matter, or the fungus that grows on it, attracts *Fungus Gnats.* You may even find them on a flowerpot or windowsill. The large Fungus Gnat has become famous in New Zealand as the "glowworm" of Waitomo Caves. Each glowing larva suspends itself close to the cave roof. It then dangles threads of secretions with sticky globules that look like a small, beaded curtain. Small flying insects are captured in this trap.

Almost every kind of plant material containing nourishment is used by flying maggots of some kind. *Seaweed Flies* lay their eggs on coarse seaweeds that are cast ashore. Similar flies live as high as 15,000 feet above sea level, on the slopes of the Himalayas. These frost-resistant maggots have only pollen grains blown from below to eat.

The *Hover Flies* are found all over the world. When approached, the Hover Fly leaps into the air, vibrating its wings. It looks like a tiny helicopter. Hover Flies are superb fliers. They place their eggs on foliage near masses of aphids (plant lice). Their maggots can then prey on the soft-bodied sapsuckers, the aphids. The Hover Fly is a friend that protects a plant from aphid attack.

Architects and Social Insects

Ants, termites, bees, and wasps live together in groups or colonies. There are rarely less than a hundred individuals in a group. The queen constructs a nest to provide protection from weather and shelter for her developing young. Successive groups mature. All of them are "workers" and are unable to reproduce young. The queen expects them to continue building the nest and caring for the brood. The workers also tend their mother, the queen. After her first brood matures, all she does is lay eggs. The workers will serve the queen for as long as the colony survives.

Termites feed on wood. The most primitive termites are in Australia. They do nothing but eat wood and gnaw galleries in fallen trees. They may eat out the heartwood from living eucalyptus trees and damage healthy fruit trees and vegetable crops.

Other termites nest in a tree, close to a reliable supply of wood. Some termites build a "carton nest" outside their tree from wood fibers cemented together with body secretions. Still others build nests that resemble massive apartment houses with dozens of inner layers and thousands of interconnected passageways.

Certain termites in Africa, like certain ants in warm places of the new world, have become farmers. They use their nests to raise fungus plants. This helps recycle vegetation faster.

Leaf-Cutter Ant

Termite queen and workers

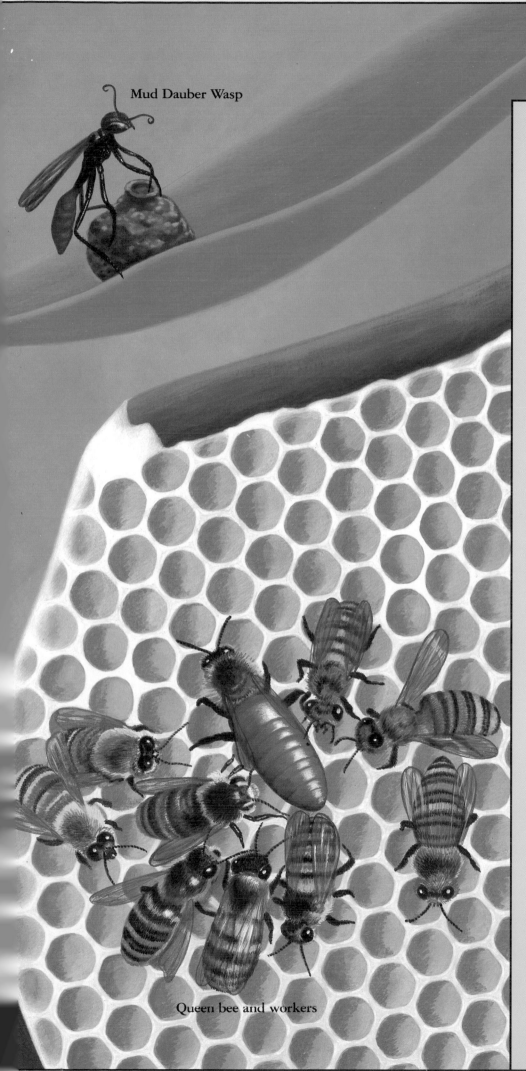

Mud Dauber Wasp

Queen bee and workers

Members of a large colony may haul home and process half a ton of plant material during their lifetime.

The *Leaf-Cutter Ants* of tropical America have similar habits. They have well-traveled trails from the nest into the forest edge. The ants climb to foliage that attracts them. Then, using a jaw like a razor blade, they cut a fragment of leaf. Clamping the leaf firmly in their jaws, they head for home. Inside their nests, Leaf-Cutters press leaf fragments into a decaying mass of vegetation, making a compost heap.

A *Mud Dauber Wasp* and a *Cicada-Killer Wasp* will each prepare an individual cell or nest first. It then goes hunting for food with which to stock it. The Mud Dauber brings back spiders, each stunned by the venom from the wasp's stinger. The Cicada-Killer Wasp hunts for cicadas instead. *Paper Wasps* of the North Temperate Zone and *Hornets* return to feed their young in brood cells with chewed-up insects.

Honeybees are masters at controlling temperature. All winter the workers cluster around their queen and keep her warm. They restore their own energy at intervals by snacking on stored honey. A colony of 50,000 bees may need fifty pounds of honey to supply them through the winter. Their nests need to be well insulated from the wind as well. They are often inside hollow trees or manmade hives.

When spring arrives, the worker Honeybees will fly forth to gather more nectar and pollen. The queen resumes her egg laying.

Weavers and Spinners

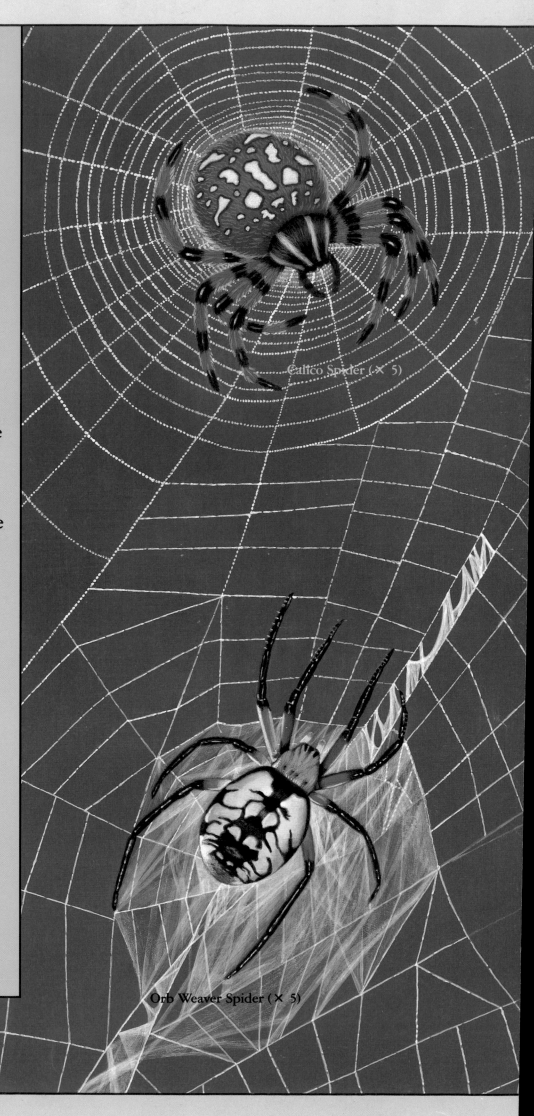

Calico Spider (× 5)

Orb Weaver Spider (× 5)

Super orb webs, six feet or more across, hang between treetops in Madagascar and other warm regions as far north as Florida. They are the work of *Calico Spiders.* These monstrous webs are incredibly strong. In fact, in countries where Calico Spiders are common, people cut the support strands and weave them into bags and baskets. Unlike many manmade fibers, they are very flexible and stay strong when wet. Some fishermen of some South Sea islands use the giant orb nets as fish nets.

Spiders make their webs at night. They rely totally on touch to do the job. All orb weavers begin with a single silken strand above the web site, called the bridge line. It must be sturdy since it will support the whole web, the spider, and her prey. We may not notice the bridge line or frame until the spider begins to spin radiating lines like the spoke of a wheel, from the frame to the center, where a hub will be. The hub area is actually a spiral of nonsticky silk. This is a free zone where she can dodge from one side of the web to another without getting stuck.

Beyond the free zone, the spider strings a single spiral strand dotted with globules of sticky glue. This is where insects will be caught and held until the spider gets to them. By nightfall the web will almost certainly be tattered and torn by insects, and by

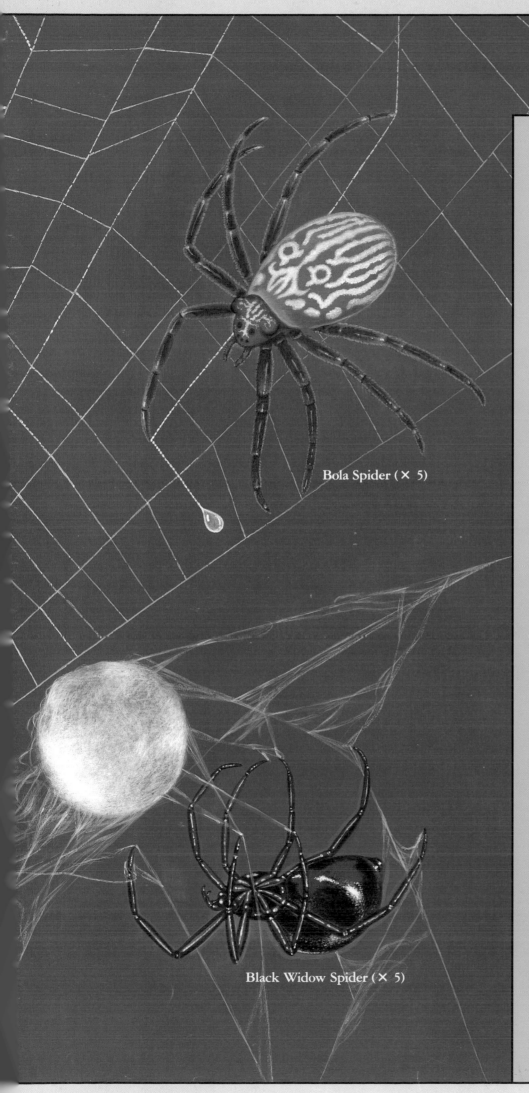

Bola Spider (× 5)

Black Widow Spider (× 5)

the spider herself as she wraps insects for later use. After dark she will eat her sticky strands and make a new web in the same place. Sometimes the spider will use the same bridge and frame lines.

On many orb webs, such as those spun by the *Black and Yellow Garden Spider,* the final feature is a zigzag strip near the center. Orb webs are one of the surest signs of spring. But by summer's end spiders no longer spin their webs. Most spiders only live from spring through summer. Only large spiders in frost-free lands are likely to survive longer. A few live a dozen years or so. However, it is unusual for a spider to live even two years.

Some of the orb weavers in the Southeastern United States seem to have lost their ability to spin webs. Instead they have become *Bola Spiders.* They stand near the top of a branch and dangle a silk line with a sticky globule at the end from one front foot. Sometimes they swing the globule in a circle. Eventually it may strike the body of a passing insect and the spider will then haul up a meal.

Indoors you often find an irregular web of sticky strands, holding dust particles. Usually this is the work of a *Cobweb Weaver,* often the *American House Spider.* Female House Spiders like to live indoors where it is warm. Adults can live indoors for more than a year. Throughout the year they hang a series of pear-shaped, brownish cocoons full of eggs in the web.

The *Black Widow* has venomous relatives over much of the world. Female Black Widows anywhere rarely leave their web, especially if it contains a pear-shaped egg mass. The mother will bite aggressively at anything that comes close unless it can escape easily. But males do not bite. After mating, the male is often eaten by the female, which is why she is called a "widow."

Most spiders rarely bite. Most are no more poisonous than a wasp sting. A great majority cannot produce sticky threads. They must get their meals without the help of webs. Some use nonsticky silk in other ways.

Early in the morning, dew makes spider webs easy to find. In short grass, you may find the work of a *Sheet-Web Weaver.* This spider is usually less than three eighths of an inch in length. Sheet-Web Weavers spin flat platform webs. They then cling to the underside of the web until the insect gets entangled in the upper surface. The little spider then pulls the insect down through the web to inject its venom. Many believe that the sheet protects the spider from spider eaters. Some species construct a second sheet below the first to protect themselves from predators on ground level. A few build tents. They then hide in the tents until something interesting bumps into the side webbing.

Funnel-Web Weaver (× 5)

Fishing Spider (× 3)

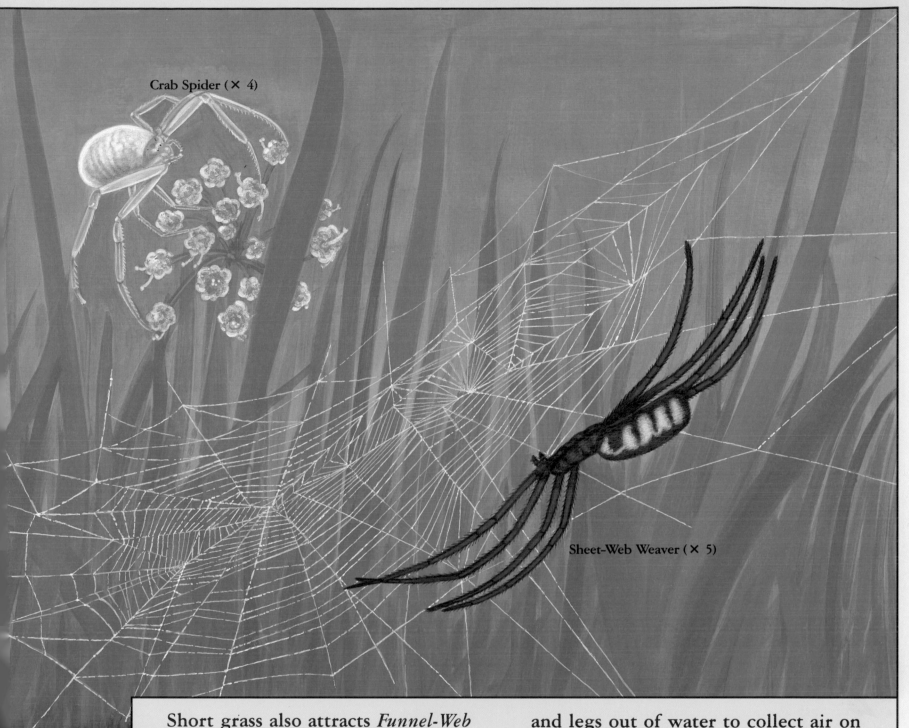

Crab Spider (× 4)

Sheet-Web Weaver (× 5)

Short grass also attracts *Funnel-Web Weavers.* These spiders spin their nonsticky sheets into a funnel-shaped pocket. They then wait. Some of these weavers create an extra web several inches higher than the main web. Flying insects will bump the web, then fall where they can be caught by the alert spider. The Funnel-Web Weaver rushes with its prey back to its lair to finish its meal.

A *European Fishing Spider* lives almost her whole life underwater, where she fashions an airtight diving bell between aquatic plants. She makes constant trips to the surface, extending her abdomen and legs out of water to collect air on her body hairs. She scrapes off the air under her diving bell. To get food for her young and herself, she creeps among the underwater plants, catching insect larvae, mites, and other prey.

The white petals of daisies and the golden ones of brown-eyed susans match the coloring of the *Crab Spider.* This lets the spider lie in ambush among the flowers, camouflaged until an insect arrives. They make no snares, retreats, or webs that remain over the winter, but provide a drag line wherever they go.

The little black and white *Zebra*

Spider is common almost anywhere in the Northern Hemisphere. Like all *Jumping Spiders,* it has keen vision. It can judge distance and leap to catch a fly ten inches away. It rarely misses its target. It spins out a silken drag line as it leaps.

The most incredible of the Jumping Spiders live 22,000 feet above sea level on the snowy slopes of Mount Everest. Many naturalists believe that the spiders are blown up so high by the strong winds. The spiders eat small flies and springtails, which feed in turn upon bits of fungus, rotting vegetation, and pollen, all wind-carried from lower levels.

Many spiders use the drag line to travel where they cannot walk. They often wait for the wind to catch the drag line and then go kiting on the wind.

A *Huntsman Spider* is too slow to travel far in any other way. Some of the big and harmless ones are welcome in Australian homes. They control household insects but make no dust-catching web.

Some huge spiders capture very large prey. In the American Southwest they are called *Tarantulas.* South Africans know these spiders as *Monkey Spiders,* and Latin Americans call them *Bird*

Zebra Spider (× 3)

Huntsman Spider (× 4)

Jumping Spider (× 4)

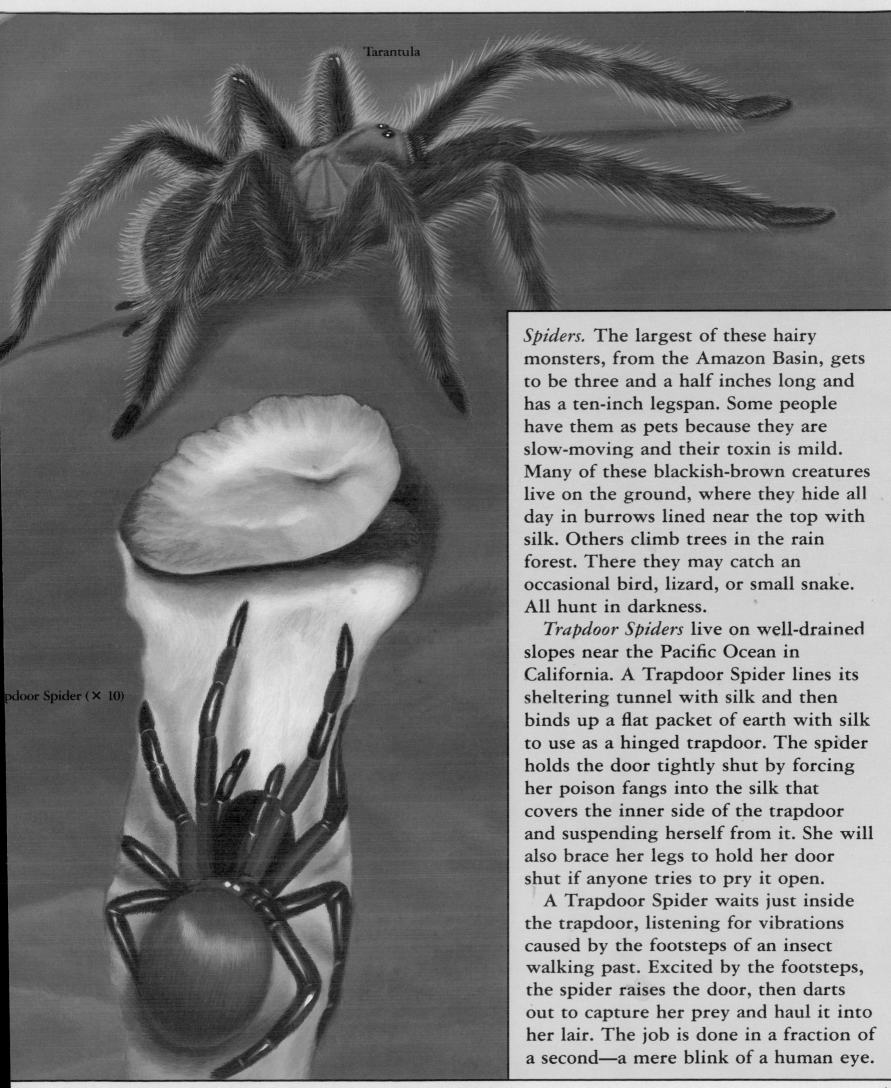

Tarantula

pdoor Spider (× 10)

Spiders. The largest of these hairy monsters, from the Amazon Basin, gets to be three and a half inches long and has a ten-inch legspan. Some people have them as pets because they are slow-moving and their toxin is mild. Many of these blackish-brown creatures live on the ground, where they hide all day in burrows lined near the top with silk. Others climb trees in the rain forest. There they may catch an occasional bird, lizard, or small snake. All hunt in darkness.

Trapdoor Spiders live on well-drained slopes near the Pacific Ocean in California. A Trapdoor Spider lines its sheltering tunnel with silk and then binds up a flat packet of earth with silk to use as a hinged trapdoor. The spider holds the door tightly shut by forcing her poison fangs into the silk that covers the inner side of the trapdoor and suspending herself from it. She will also brace her legs to hold her door shut if anyone tries to pry it open.

A Trapdoor Spider waits just inside the trapdoor, listening for vibrations caused by the footsteps of an insect walking past. Excited by the footsteps, the spider raises the door, then darts out to capture her prey and haul it into her lair. The job is done in a fraction of a second—a mere blink of a human eye.

Insects Sharing the Environment

Insects and spiders share their world with plants and other animals, and with humankind as well. We already know that these small creatures have been a constructive force on Earth.

Insects do more to help other kinds of life than they do to use up the Earth's resources. We cannot say the same for ourselves. We have done much to deplete the Earth's resources and damage many environments. Now we are becoming aware of the consequences.

Humankind need not feel overwhelmed by the more than 600,000 kinds of insects. Individually they may number at least 10,000,000,000,000,000,000 (10 quintillion), yet relatively few have an adverse impact on human welfare as long as we do not try to manage the environment solely for our benefit. If so many unthinking insects can perform so well, surely intelligent human beings can learn from them to share the world successfully. Destruction of the rain forests and other environments could mean destruction of the beneficial insects and spiders, making way for the less favorable creatures. The cockroach may outlive humans and continue its successful ways.

House Spider (× 10)

Cockroach (× 2)

Index

About the Authors

Lorus J. Milne and Margery Milne, each with a Ph.D. in biology, were long active on the faculty of the University of New Hampshire system. They have combined a life of teaching with writing on natural history subjects; in all, they have coauthored close to fifty books, for adults and for young people. Their field studies have taken them across North America, Central America, the West Indies, Africa, Asia, Australia, and more—altogether well over a million miles.

About the Artist

Claire Phipps was born in Argentina and trained in oil painting at the University of Fine Arts in Budapest. She has painted portraits and worked in textile design, and has always been fascinated by the beauty of everything in nature—including insects and spiders. She has two children and lives in New Haven, Connecticut.

Grasshopper molting and emerging as adult